UN Security Council Enlargement and U.S. Interests

COUNCIL *on* FOREIGN RELATIONS

International Institutions and Global Governance Program

Council Special Report No. 59
December 2010

Kara C. McDonald and Stewart M. Patrick

UN Security Council Enlargement and U.S. Interests

The Council on Foreign Relations (CFR) is an independent, nonpartisan membership organization, think tank, and publisher dedicated to being a resource for its members, government officials, business executives, journalists, educators and students, civic and religious leaders, and other interested citizens in order to help them better understand the world and the foreign policy choices facing the United States and other countries. Founded in 1921, the Council carries out its mission by maintaining a diverse membership, with special programs to promote interest and develop expertise in the next generation of foreign policy leaders; convening meetings at its headquarters in New York and in Washington, DC, and other cities where senior government officials, members of Congress, global leaders, and prominent thinkers come together with Council members to discuss and debate major international issues; supporting a Studies Program that fosters independent research, enabling Council scholars to produce articles, reports, and books and hold roundtables that analyze foreign policy issues and make concrete policy recommendations; publishing *Foreign Affairs*, the preeminent journal on international affairs and U.S. foreign policy; sponsoring Independent Task Forces that produce reports with both findings and policy prescriptions on the most important foreign policy topics; and providing up-to-date information and analysis about world events and American foreign policy on its website, CFR.org.

The Council on Foreign Relations takes no institutional positions on policy issues and has no affiliation with the U.S. government. All statements of fact and expressions of opinion contained in its publications are the sole responsibility of the author or authors.

Council Special Reports (CSRs) are concise policy briefs, produced to provide a rapid response to a developing crisis or contribute to the public's understanding of current policy dilemmas. CSRs are written by individual authors—who may be CFR fellows or acknowledged experts from outside the institution—in consultation with an advisory committee, and are intended to take sixty days from inception to publication. The committee serves as a sounding board and provides feedback on a draft report. It usually meets twice—once before a draft is written and once again when there is a draft for review; however, advisory committee members, unlike Task Force members, are not asked to sign off on the report or to otherwise endorse it. Once published, CSRs are posted on www.cfr.org.

For further information about CFR or this Special Report, please write to the Council on Foreign Relations, 58 East 68th Street, New York, NY 10065, or call the Communications office at 212.434.9888. Visit our website, www.cfr.org.

Printed in the United States of America.

To submit a letter in response to a Council Special Report for publication on our website, CFR.org, you may send an email to CSReditor@cfr.org. Alternatively, letters may be mailed to us at: Publications Department, Council on Foreign Relations, 58 East 68th Street, New York, NY 10065. Letters should include the writer's name, postal address, and daytime phone number. Letters may be edited for length and clarity, and may be published online. Please do not send attachments. All letters become the property of the Council on Foreign Relations and will not be returned. We regret that, owing to the volume of correspondence, we cannot respond to every letter.

This report is printed on paper that is certified by SmartWood to the standards of the Forest Stewardship Council, which promotes environmentally responsible, socially beneficial, and economically viable management of the world's forests.

FSC
Mixed Sources
Product group from well-managed forests and other controlled sources
www.fsc.org Cert no. SW-COC-001530
© 1996 Forest Stewardship Council

Contents

Foreword

The United Nations Security Council (UNSC) remains an important source of legitimacy for international action. Yet despite dramatic changes in the international system over the past forty-five years, the composition of the UNSC has remained unaltered since 1965, and there are many who question how long its legitimacy will last without additional members that reflect twenty-first-century realities. There is little agreement, however, as to which countries should accede to the Security Council or even by what formula aspirants should be judged. Reform advocates frequently call for equal representation for various regions of the world, but local competitors like India and Pakistan or Mexico and Brazil are unlikely to reach a compromise solution. Moreover, the UN Charter prescribes that regional parity should be, at most, a secondary issue; the ability to advocate and defend international peace and security should, it says, be the primary concern.

The United States has remained largely silent as this debate has intensified over the past decade, choosing to voice general support for expansion without committing to specifics. (President Barack Obama's recent call for India to become a permanent member of the Security Council was a notable exception.) In this Council Special Report, 2009–2010 International Affairs Fellow Kara C. McDonald and Senior Fellow Stewart M. Patrick argue that American reticence is ultimately unwise. Rather than merely observing the discussions on this issue, they believe that the United States should take the lead. To do so, they advocate a criteria-based process that will gauge aspirant countries on a variety of measures, including political stability, the capacity and willingness to act in defense of international security, the ability to negotiate and implement sometimes unpopular agreements, and the institutional wherewithal to participate in a demanding UNSC agenda. They further recommend that this process be initiated and implemented with early and regular input from Congress; detailed advice from relevant

Executive agencies as to which countries should be considered and on what basis; careful, private negotiations in aspirant capitals; and the interim use of alternate multilateral forums such as the Group of Twenty (G20) to satisfy countries' immediate demands for broader participation and to produce evidence about their willingness and ability to participate constructively in the international system.

The issues facing the world in the twenty-first century—climate change, terrorism, economic development, nonproliferation, and more—will demand a great deal of the multilateral system. The United States will have little to gain from the dilution or rejection of UNSC authority. In *UN Security Council Enlargement and U.S. Interests*, McDonald and Patrick outline sensible reforms to protect the efficiency and utility of the existing Security Council while expanding it to incorporate new global actors. Given the growing importance of regional powers and the myriad challenges facing the international system, their report provides a strong foundation for future action.

Richard N. Haass
President
Council on Foreign Relations
December 2010

Acknowledgments

One of the great pleasures in writing this report was the opportunity to speak with leading experts on the past, present, and possible future of the UN Security Council. Above all, we thank the members of our advisory committee for their energetic participation in deliberations, including their extensive, thoughtful comments on previous drafts. We are especially grateful to the committee chair, Ambassador R. Nicholas Burns, who lent his intelligence, grace, and imagination to the enterprise.

We are indebted to CFR President Richard N. Haass and Director of Studies James M. Lindsay for their decision to approve this project, and for their careful reading of the manuscript.

In the course of this project, we conducted background interviews with numerous officials from UN member states. These meetings, held on a not-for-attribution basis, helped illuminate the current diplomatic landscape and avenues for navigating its topography. Several U.S. government offices also provided useful statistics and factual information. Richard Gowan provided detailed comments on the manuscript.

This report rests on the hard work of dedicated CFR staff whose names do not appear on the title page. Farah Faisal Thaler, Shelby Leighton, and Dani Cinali provided invaluable research assistance; Preeti Bhattacharji made our prose concise and coherent; Patricia Dorff and Lia Norton ensured that our work was presentable; and Kaysie Brown supervised this project as deputy director of the International Institutions and Global Governance (IIGG) program.

This publication was made possible by the generous support of the Robina Foundation. We are grateful to the foundation for its commitment to support new thinking about international cooperation. Kara would also like to thank CFR's International Affairs Fellowship

Program and the U.S. Department of State for permitting a year of research and writing at the Council on Foreign Relations.

The views expressed herein are those of the authors, and do not necessarily reflect the views of the U.S. Department of State or the U.S. government.

Kara C. McDonald
Stewart M. Patrick

Acronyms

DPKO	UN Department of Peacekeeping Operations
E10	ten elected members of the UN Security Council
ECOSOC	UN Economic and Social Council
G4	Group of Four (Brazil, Germany, India, Japan)
G20	Group of Twenty
G77	Group of Seventy-Seven
NAM	Nonaligned Movement
NATO	North Atlantic Treaty Organization
NSC	U.S. National Security Council
OEWG	Open-ended Working Group
P5	five permanent members of the UN Security Council (China, France, Russia, United Kingdom, United States)
UfC	Uniting for Consensus (Argentina, Canada, Italy, Malta, Mexico, Pakistan, South Korea, Spain, Turkey)
UNGA	UN General Assembly
UNSC	UN Security Council

Council Special Report

Introduction

Advancing U.S. national interests in an era of global threats depends on effective multilateral action. Global institutions inherited from the past are struggling to adapt to the rise of new challenges and powers. "The international architecture of the 20th century is buckling," declares the new U.S. National Security Strategy.[1] President Barack Obama has committed his administration to renovating outdated institutions and integrating emerging powers as pillars of a rule-based international order.[2] Renovation of the United Nations Security Council (UNSC) and its membership must be a core component of this agenda. President Obama's announcement in November 2010 of U.S. support for a permanent UNSC seat for India is a critical first step in this direction.

Few subjects arouse as much passion as the question of altering the size of the UNSC. The reason is obvious. Debates about the UNSC's composition are about core issues of global power. The UN Charter establishes the UNSC as the premier international watchdog, designates the five permanent members (P5) as guarantors of global peace, and endows each with a veto. Although imperfect, the UNSC is indispensable to the pursuit of U.S. national security and the maintenance of world order. But it is also increasingly outdated, its composition unchanged since 1965. To date, competing reform proposals, which have focused exclusively on enlarging the UNSC in an effort to broaden buy-in, have emerged from competing coalitions, but none has come close to the support needed to amend the UN Charter.

President Obama claims to have renewed U.S. leadership at the United Nations. Yet until his surprise announcement of support for India's candidacy, his administration remained guarded on updating the UNSC. Such reticence is understandable. While many U.S. officials believe that the UNSC no longer reflects global power realities, they disagree over whether any plausible enlargement would benefit U.S. national interests or strengthen the UNSC's function. Common justifications for UNSC reform (based on equitable representation, regional entitlement, and a purported identity crisis) are simply unpersuasive, and much depends on the behavior of aspirant countries once on the UNSC. Even if change is desirable, some wonder whether the United States can possibly effectuate it in such a complex diplomatic landscape—or if it should assume the considerable risks of spearheading the effort.

A more compelling reason to support UNSC enlargement, however, is concern that an unchanged UNSC will become increasingly ineffective in addressing today's security challenges, which demand cohesive, broad-based multilateral responses. The Security Council is not in immediate crisis, but neither is the status quo indefinitely sustainable. The United States—still the world's most influential nation—has a window of opportunity to break the current logjam by advancing a clear vision of a renovated Security Council capable of implementing its mandate in an era of transnational threats.

President Obama should build on his India announcement by publicly supporting a UNSC expansion, laying out a long-term road map to incorporate several major aspirant countries to new permanent seats, based on concrete criteria commensurate with the weighty obligations of membership. By shifting the acrimonious debate from claims of entitlement toward a conditions-based, evolutionary process, the United States can avoid reform schemes contrary to its interests. It can also ensure a reform that demands that aspirants accept the responsibilities—not just the privileges—of power. This prudent course would avoid the considerable risks of immediate UNSC enlargement, while giving aspirants an incentive to increase their contributions to global security. By advocating for this agenda, the United States takes the moral high ground—which could pay diplomatic dividends, whether enlargement occurs or not—and works toward an expansion that improves, rather than reduces, the long-term effectiveness of the UNSC.

The Case for Enlargement

The UN Security Council was created after the most destructive war in history to help the world respond to global security threats—with overwhelming force if needed. The UN Charter, as amended in 1965, creates a fifteen-member council with the authority to impose binding decisions on all UN member states. The UNSC's power resides with the five permanent members—China, France, Russia, the United Kingdom, and the United States—designated in 1945 as the primary guardians of world order. The charter makes no mention of geographic representation as a consideration for permanent membership, but provides ten additional seats elected for two-year terms based on contributions to peace and security, with consideration to geographic parity (in practice the elected seats have been divvied up among the regional blocs).[3]

Proponents of enlargement observe that the distribution of global power has changed dramatically since 1945, and that the number of UN member states has surged from 51 to 192 without a parallel expansion of the UNSC. The UNSC's permanent membership, for example, excludes major UN funders like Japan and Germany, emerging powers like India and Brazil, and all of Africa and Latin America. Enlargement proponents warn that the UNSC's global authority will erode if it fails to expand membership from underrepresented regions. Moreover, skillfully accomplished enlargement could provide a near-term opportunity to manage power transitions, "socializing" today's regional leaders into "responsible" global actors that shoulder a greater share of international security. If expansion is inevitable, proponents believe, the United States should lead it now—when it retains unparalleled ability to shape the terms of the debate—rather than get dragged along by others later.

Opponents of enlargement dispute that the UNSC is experiencing a crisis of legitimacy, arguing that it remains the most effective of all

UN organs and that the UNSC's permanent structure still reflects the leading political and military powers. Enlargement would dilute U.S. power, increase gridlock, encourage lowest-common-denominator actions, and empower antagonistic leaders of the nonaligned movement (NAM). The expectation that permanent UNSC membership will tame obstreperous state behavior at the UN is naive, and championing reform prior to confidence-building among—and demonstrated responsible behavior by—regional leaders could be disastrous.[4] In any case, UNSC reform is unlikely to be achieved, given the two-thirds United Nations General Assembly (UNGA) and unanimous P5 support required for charter revision. The United States would thus be foolish to take the lead on UNSC reform, which would only alienate the main aspirants or the next tier of countries—many of which are U.S. allies. It would be wiser to let multilateral negotiations continue along an inconclusive path than risk blame for a failed negotiation or conclude a reform that jeopardizes U.S. interest.

A CLOSER LOOK

A closer look suggests that while many arguments often offered in support of enlargement are flawed, the case for expanding the UN Security Council is a compelling one. A common claim, particularly in the developing world, is that the UNSC is increasingly illegitimate and ineffective, given its inequitable geographic composition, declining relevance to today's security threats, inability to ensure compliance with its ostensibly binding resolutions, and exclusion of countries that could contribute to international security. According to this analysis, the UNSC is in poor and even terminal condition.

In truth, the situation is nowhere near so dire. The actual behavior of member states, as opposed to their rhetoric, suggests the UNSC's legitimacy, credibility, and effectiveness are more robust than critics claim. Nevertheless, failure to enlarge the UNSC is problematic, for it excludes from permanent membership powerful countries that could contribute to international security and offer long-term political support for the United Nations.

DWINDLING LEGITIMACY?

From the perspective of the United States and other permanent members, the legitimacy of the UNSC as currently constituted is clear: it emanates from the UN Charter. As long as the charter remains in force and unamended, the existing UNSC structure is legitimate.

To date, critiques of the UNSC's legitimacy have been couched primarily in terms of equitable geographic representation. According to regional blocs, the UNSC's domination by Western countries and failure to include permanent members from Africa and Latin America give it dwindling authority to issue binding international decisions, particularly in settings like sub-Saharan Africa, where the majority of UN peace operations occur.[5] The lack of perspectives from the global South reinforces perceptions that the UNSC is a neocolonial club, determining questions of war and peace for the poor without their input.

Such talking points pack a political punch in the developing world. But these arguments confront two inconvenient truths. First, regional representation and parity were never the basis for designating the UNSC's permanent members, which were chosen primarily as guarantors of world peace. The same should be true, presumably, of any additional permanent seats. The charter suggests that the candidacies of emerging powers such as Brazil or India (as well as established ones like Germany and Japan) should be weighed not on their role as regional leaders, but on their ability to help safeguard international peace. The place to address regional balance is clearly in the UNSC's elected seats, since Article 23 of the UN Charter explicitly mentions "equitable geographic distribution" as a secondary consideration.

Second, designating new permanent members will not likely sate demands for greater regional representation. Indeed, opposition to the main aspirants (Brazil, Germany, India, and Japan) is strongest from their regional rivals (Argentina, Mexico, Italy, Pakistan, and South Korea). Some propose that each regional bloc should determine its own permanent representative, but such decisions are more properly left to the entire world body. Regional selection could result in the seating of unexpected, possibly compromising candidates. Should the United States accept Cuba or Venezuela as a permanent UNSC member if, by some bizarre twist in backroom negotiations, Brazil or Mexico cannot secure Latin American support?

DECREASING RELEVANCE?

The UNSC's relevance is not declining; it remains the premier multilateral institution for matters of international security. To be sure, UN member states exploit a range of frameworks—including regional organizations, ad hoc coalitions, and interest-based partnerships—to advance their national and collective security. Examples range from the African Union to the Six Party Talks on North Korea. But in the last five years, the UNSC has spent comparatively less time rubber-stamping diplomatic agreements made outside its chambers and more time forging agreements within its own ranks. UNSC Resolution 1701 to end the Lebanon war, the P5+ Germany negotiations on Iran, and the UNSC's sanctions against North Korea are all examples. The UNSC's continued relevance is also illustrated by states' desire to serve on it. Every October, the UNGA is filled to capacity when delegations elect the new rotating UNSC members amid an orgy of vote-buying. Even countries that make a profession of attacking the UNSC's credibility nonetheless spend millions trying to gain a seat—suggesting that, at a minimum, it retains prestige.[6]

WEAKENING IMPLEMENTATION?

Some critics claim that the lack of geographic balance in the council's permanent membership and its failure to include regional leaders erode its perceived authority, complicating the implementation and enforcement of its resolutions, and causing states to turn to other frameworks to address security problems.

With rare exceptions, however, UN members continue to regard the UNSC as the most authoritative international institution in matters of global peace and security. To be sure, states are sometimes slow to align national laws and practices with new UNSC resolutions, and bureaucratic inertia contributes to deficiencies in implementation. But the resolutions most commonly flouted today are those imposing sanctions and other punitive measures, and the violators tend to be the targeted states and their sympathizers. These are cases less of weak implementation than of political defiance. Examples include the arms embargoes on Sudan and Somalia, resolutions condemning violence in eastern Congo, and the sanctions resolutions against Iran and North Korea. A change in UNSC composition would probably not address noncompliance by offending states, like North Korea, Iran, or Syria.

A MORE COMPELLING CASE FOR REFORM: SHIFTING CONCEPTS AND REALITIES OF POWER

The UNSC, then, faces no immediate crisis of legitimacy, credibility, or relevance. At the same time, however, there is a powerful geopolitical argument for compositional reform. The primary consideration for permanent membership should be power—the ability and willingness to deploy it in service of global security. Openness to UNSC enlargement is justified by the changing nature of threats to international peace and by the need to harness the power of emerging and established states as pillars of an open, rule-bound global system.

In 1945, permanent UNSC membership was primarily justified by political-military power, including a capacity to prevent—and, if necessary, conduct and win—interstate war.[7] But in today's more diffuse security environment, national military power is no longer the sole or necessarily supreme qualification. Combating transnational threats, ranging from terrorism to nuclear proliferation to climate change, requires not only military but also diplomatic, economic, and technological capabilities.[8] Strategies to contain, manage, and solve global challenges depend as much on the cohesion of multilateral responses as on military might—and they require the contributions of all major emerging and established powers.

In this new environment, the relevant question is: What composition does the UNSC need to fulfill its mandate to maintain international peace and security? The past six decades have witnessed significant shifts in the relative size of the world's largest economies, alongside more modest shifts in relative defense spending (see Appendix 1). These trends suggest the emergence of new countries able to contribute to international peace and security. The hurdle to UNSC permanent membership must remain high, and aspirant countries should demonstrate an ability to broker and deliver global solutions to transnational threats.

Skillfully accomplished, UNSC expansion could be an investment in global stability. While the UNSC is not presently in crisis, there are persuasive practical and geopolitical grounds for the United States to support a modest enlargement of its permanent membership. To fulfill its mandate the UNSC needs to draw on the collective authority and capabilities of many states. The Obama administration has an opportunity to shift the reform debate from one of entitlement to one of responsibility and action. Such an institutional bargain may appear at first magnanimous, but actually reflects enlightened self-interest.[9] By spearheading reform that gives emerging nations (as well as important established powers) a stake in the current order, the United States can increase global political support for (or at least acquiescence to) existing arrangements and leverage the contributions of capable states willing to provide a larger share of global public goods.

Historically, the task of accommodating rising powers has been among the most difficult challenges of world politics. International relations tend to be particularly turbulent when the global distribution of power changes and international structures fail to keep pace. The interwar years (1919–39) provide a case in point.[10] While it is impossible to predict the future, failure to adjust the UNSC's composition could well complicate multilateral security cooperation in the decades ahead. The most dire scenario—that dissatisfied states might launch a full-scale assault on the UNSC's legitimacy and seek to undermine its role—seems unlikely. More plausible is that frustrated aspirants could reduce their investments in—and diplomatic support for—the institution, depriving the UNSC of needed capabilities and reducing its overall effectiveness.

Any effort to enlarge the UNSC will be difficult, but it will get harder with time as power diffuses around the world and calls for reform increase. By acting now, the United States can help harness the capabilities of new global actors and create incentives for their responsible behavior.

The Tough Diplomatic Landscape

Any discussion of UNSC enlargement must include a sober appreciation of the hurdles to revising the UN Charter, the present horn-locked diplomatic landscape, and the obstacles even a determined United States would face in bringing about such a reform.

AMENDING THE CHARTER

Amending the UN Charter is an onerous process, requiring not only approval of two-thirds of the UNGA, but also ratification of the relevant domestic legislation by two-thirds of UN member states (including all of the P5).[11] The charter has been revised only three times in sixty-five years, including in 1965, when the UNSC expanded from eleven to fifteen by adding four elected members (see Appendix 2).[12]

Amending the charter faces a multitude of obstacles, not least within the U.S. Congress. Any UN Charter amendment would require bipartisan backing on Capitol Hill. At present, support in Congress for the United Nations is irresolute, and past bipartisan legislation has linked payment of UN dues to management reform. U.S. legislators may well insist on the implementation of system-wide UN reforms prior to supporting UNSC expansion.[13] Nevertheless, recent polls suggest U.S. public support for a modest expansion of the UNSC's permanent membership, including seats for Germany, Japan, Brazil, and India.[14]

PAST REFORM EFFORTS

In the UNGA, the issue of UNSC enlargement has been a perennial source of debate for the last thirty years. It first appeared on the UNGA agenda in 1979,[15] but the first credible push for UNSC reform came during the run-up to the UN World Summit in September 2005, when UN secretary-general Kofi Annan proposed two models for UNSC expansion.[16] This prompted the major negotiating blocs—the so-called Group of Four (or G4, composed of Brazil, Germany, India, and Japan), the Uniting for Consensus (UfC) coalition, and the African Union—to propose their own models of expansion (see Appendix 4). Ultimately, none of the major coalitions gained anything close to a two-thirds UNGA majority during the UN High-level Event in September 2005.[17]

In September 2008, the UNGA shifted discussions of UNSC reform from the consensus-based Open-ended Working Group (OEWG) to intergovernmental negotiations in the UNGA plenary.[18] This raised the prospect that an enlargement resolution might actually be brought to a vote. Through October 2010, UN member states had held five negotiating sessions, which revealed that a majority of UN member states favor an expansion of both permanent and elected UNSC members. Despite this shift, the impasse in New York persists, with the major camps reciting well-known positions—none of which enjoys support from two-thirds of the UNGA—and with each camp's fallback remaining the status quo. No breakthrough seems likely absent compromises in each group's current stance—and leadership from the United States.

CURRENT ATTITUDES OF THE PERMANENT MEMBERS

Among permanent members, France is most enthusiastic about enlargement, followed by the United Kingdom.[19] This public stance may be motivated by the growing vulnerability of their own permanent seats, given perceptions that Europe is overrepresented among the P5. Indeed, the Lisbon Treaty increases pressure to consolidate the two nations' membership into a single seat for the European Union, something neither seems prepared to contemplate.

In March 2008, France and Britain jointly proposed creating an "interim" category of longer-term, renewable seats, to be held by a handful of countries, notionally for five to fifteen years. (At present, a country cannot serve consecutive elected terms.) This period would be followed by a review conference on final status. Reactions from the G4 have been mixed, with India most adamantly opposed. Unsurprisingly, each major coalition has in turn offered its own, self-serving interpretation of this "interim" option. Some regard it as a temporary status leading to permanent membership; others as an enduring "intermediate" category that eliminates the prospect of additional permanent seats.

Russia, sensitive to any decline in relative power, opposes additional permanent members and efforts to qualify the P5 veto. China says it is open to UNSC expansion, including additional elected members from Africa, but will likely resist any new permanent members (with particular animus to adding Japan and, increasingly, regional rival India). Chinese officials argue that adding permanent members would only exacerbate representation issues and antagonize the next tier of countries. China has signaled openness to the "intermediate" approach, but may consider it a step to defer G4 ambitions.

CURRENT U.S. POLICY

Despite its rhetorical commitment to updating international institutions, the Obama administration, like administrations before it, has shied from leadership on UNSC reform. Rather than advance a particular proposal, U.S. officials have offered broad statements in support of a limited expansion of both permanent and nonpermanent members within five parameters. These statements include:

- enlargement cannot diminish the UNSC's effectiveness or efficiency;[20]
- any proposal to expand permanent membership must name specific countries (ruling out so-called framework proposals);[21]
- candidates for permanent membership must be judged on their ability to contribute to the maintenance of international peace and security;
- there should be no changes to the current veto structure; and
- expansion proposals must accommodate charter requirements for ratification, including approval by two-thirds of the U.S. Senate.[22]

The Obama administration's stance presents only two modest changes to that of its predecessor. First, it no longer conditions movement on UNSC expansion to progress on broader UN management and budgetary reform. Second, whereas the Bush administration supported only Japan's candidacy, the Obama administration has announced support for India as an additional permanent member, leaving other potential configurations open for discussion.[23]

Beyond these parameters, the Obama administration has not proposed any specific reforms, clarified the acceptable limits of any expansion, or endorsed any candidates.[24] President Obama has not launched an interagency review of the matter, and aspirant countries have not yet pressed him vigorously on it. Whether the time has come to alter the UNSC's composition—and, if so, how it should be altered—remain subjects of fierce debate.

U.S. Interests in UNSC Enlargement

That both Democratic and Republican administrations have adopted roughly similar policies on UNSC reform suggests a common assessment of the risks and likely rewards. For Washington, an ideal enlargement scenario might be simply adding the G4 powers as permanent (or long-term) members without veto power. The resulting UNSC of nineteen would ensure the United States of at least two reliable allies (Germany and Japan), and possibly others (Brazil and India) depending on the issue. Such a modest enlargement would also be consistent with the original purpose of the UNSC as a privileged body of great powers capable of sustaining global peace. At present, however, this scheme is unlikely to win support from two-thirds of the UNGA without concessions to Africa.

For the United States, "interim" options could also provide a testing ground for aspirants to demonstrate their leadership and qualifications before a decision is made on their permanent status. A critical question, though, is who will have the power to select the slate of countries—and to determine whether their seats are renewed or (potentially) made permanent. Granting such authority to regional groups (or even to the UNGA) could fuel regional constituency dynamics and encourage aspirants to satisfy their blocs to gain reelection, rather than exhibiting the independence necessary to represent global responsibilities.

THE UNITED STATES' STAKES IN AN EFFECTIVE UN SECURITY COUNCIL

The United States pursues its national objectives through a wide array of multilateral bodies, ranging from the North Atlantic Treaty Organization (NATO) to the Group of Twenty (G20). Yet the United Nations is unique in its universality, convening power, technical capacity, and perceived legitimacy. These strengths are not easily or consistently replicated in other formats, be they military alliances, regional organizations, consultative forums, or ad hoc coalitions.

The UN's main institutional strength is its ability to balance the egalitarian principle of sovereign equality—as embodied in the 192-member General Assembly—with the hierarchical reality of global power, as reflected in the fifteen-member Security Council. While the UNGA provides a forum in which all states have an equal vote and can express their views, the UNSC serves as the preeminent decision- and law-making body on matters of international peace and security—one in which the United States retains preeminent influence.

The United States regularly resorts to the UNSC to gain political backing and legal authority for multilateral initiatives that advance U.S. objectives. Over the past several years, the United States has sought and obtained sanctions resolutions against Iran for violations of its Nuclear Nonproliferation Treaty obligations, as well as to isolate the North Korean regime of Kim Jong-Il. It has relied on the UNSC to authorize or renew missions in Afghanistan and Iraq, to strengthen controls on the illicit spread of nuclear weapons, and to sanction terrorist organizations. It has also turned to the UNSC to share the burdens, risks, and responsibilities of intervening in conflicts in which U.S. interests support a response, but in which competing priorities, lack of resources, or political circumstances militate against high-profile U.S. involvement. The UN's Department of Peacekeeping Operations (DPKO) now fields the world's second-largest expeditionary force, with 114,000 personnel deployed in seventeen operations, from Haiti to Sudan.[25] The United States recognizes that the benefits of the UN's international peacekeeping apparatus are well worth its investment.[26]

UNITED STATES' VIEWS ON UNSC EFFECTIVENESS

Despite the stakes, the UNSC can frustrate U.S. diplomats when it proves unwilling to act, does so only belatedly, or fails to enforce its decisions. Failure to act quickly often indicates P5 disagreement over what actions, if any, should be taken. The United States, Great Britain, and France (the so-called P3) are often at loggerheads with Russia and China, for instance, on how forcefully to respond to Iran's nuclear ambitions, with the former typically taking a much harder line. Although the veto is rarely used, its very existence means some draft resolutions are never tabled or brought to a vote, or are replaced with more diluted statements.[27] Generating support for decisive action among the UNSC's ten elected members (or E10) can also be difficult, given the propensity of some delegations to adopt positions that curry favor with the Group of Seventy-Seven (G77) or their regional blocs.

Equally frustrating to U.S. interests is the invocation of state sovereignty to stymie UNSC intervention in the face of gross human rights violations, as in the cases of Myanmar, Sri Lanka, Sudan, and Zimbabwe. Indeed, some elected members express general opposition to the use of any coercive measures, namely sanctions and military force—the very tools that provide the UNSC's unique powers.

Finally, while UNSC resolutions are binding on all states, there are few enforcement mechanisms beyond public shaming when states do not uphold their obligations. The four UN sanctions resolutions against Iran and two against North Korea, for instance, are among the strongest multilateral sanctions regimes ever adopted, but they lack teeth.[28] Beyond the targets themselves, the broader UN membership—including at times UNSC members—are known to violate resolutions by trading in banned goods with sanctioned countries.

No conceivable UNSC reform can eliminate competition or homogenize state preferences, but U.S. officials must consider the extent to which reforms would exacerbate or quell these sometimes maddening dynamics. Given diverse threat perceptions, the UNSC will remain an imperfect and selective system of collective security.[29] A more realistic (though still daunting) U.S. objective would be to negotiate a change in UNSC composition that aligns national interests more frequently and generates responses to today's security challenges.

THE EFFECT OF UNSC REFORM ON UNSC EFFECTIVENESS

The case for expansion is often couched in terms of legitimacy, conceived as a function of how representative the body is of the broader UN membership. This has encouraged more debate over the right size and geographic parity of an enlarged UNSC, rather than about how effective it would be in performing its mandate. A close analysis suggests that expanding the UNSC would likely hinder its efficiency, but its impact on UNSC effectiveness is more difficult to predict. It depends on how big the enlargement is, what form it takes, and, most importantly, which countries are selected.

Enlargement would certainly complicate U.S. tactics in negotiations, particularly in lining up votes for important resolutions. Larger bodies are often more hesitant to take decisive action, vulnerable to blockage, and susceptible to lowest-common-denominator decision-making. In the current fifteen-member body, it takes seven votes to block an agenda item and nine votes with no vetoes to pass a resolution.[30] Already, U.S. ability to form winning coalitions on the UNSC varies with the cohort of elected members.[31] Any enlargement would require negotiating critical new thresholds, and the United States must consider at what point a body becomes too unwieldy to fulfill its mandate.

It is hard to predict how these dynamics would change in an enlarged UNSC. But the hurdles for mobilizing winning or blocking coalitions would clearly be higher.[32] In a UNSC of twenty-one members, for example, thirteen votes would presumably be needed for a positive vote, nine to block.[33] Vote counting becomes more complicated as numbers grow, creating an opportunity for a determined group of elected members to exercise a collective veto over UNSC decisions. This is problematic, as the most popular proposals for enlargement call for a UNSC of twenty-four or twenty-five (including several new elected members).

Adding new permanent members—or creating a new tier of longer-term or renewable seats—could also make the diplomatic landscape unpredictable. Coalitions could coalesce and dissolve according to issue areas, regional interests, or ideological affinity. Some new members—Germany and Japan, say—might align more closely with the United States, France, and the United Kingdom, while others might make common cause with China and Russia. Alternatively, negotiations could become tri-tiered, moving from the veto-wielding P5 to the rest of the long-term members before ending with the full UNSC.

ASSESSING LIKELY ASPIRANT BEHAVIOR

But certainly which states are around the table is just as important as how many. The presence of new, proactive permanent members could inspire collective action and marshal the capabilities of rising actors.

Much then depends on new-member behavior. Will such countries embrace global responsibilities and adopt policies broadly consistent with the U.S. worldview, or will they import bloc agendas and pursue narrow national interests?

An optimistic scenario imagines that the most likely candidates—Germany, Japan, Brazil, India, and perhaps South Africa—would tend to align with the United States as democracies, inclining the UNSC's balance of power in Washington's direction. A more skeptical assessment predicts that India, Brazil, and South Africa—three leaders of the nonaligned and G77 voting bloc—would use their newfound status to ramp up anti-U.S. discourse in the UNSC, diverging from Western ideals on critical issues like human rights and nonproliferation.

The recent performance of major developing countries as elected members of the UNSC is mixed. During its controversial 2007–2008 tenure on the UNSC, for example, South Africa used its position as a regional leader to weaken UNSC action on Sudan and impede discussion of wide-scale human rights abuses in Zimbabwe and Myanmar. Likewise, both Brazil and Turkey voted against a fourth round of UNSC sanctions on Iran in June 2010. UNGA voting patterns also provide grounds for caution. Unlike Japan and Germany, which are most closely aligned with U.S. preferences, Brazil, India, and South Africa frequently vote contrary to U.S. preferences, showing that close bilateral relations do not always translate into cooperation in multilateral settings (see Appendix 3).

Ideally, developing countries elevated to positions of authority would seriously weigh their responsibilities for global security, abandoning the aspects of G77 and NAM diplomacy that often turn the UNGA into a circus. In his inaugural address to the UNGA in September 2009, President Obama spoke wistfully of the need to discard outdated bloc affiliations:

> The traditional division between nations of the South and the North makes no sense in an interconnected world; nor do alignments rooted in the cleavages of a long-gone Cold War. The time has come to realize that the old habits, the old arguments, are irrelevant to the challenges faced by our people.[34]

But old habits die hard. India is a case in point. India has close relations with the United States, but in the UNGA, the UN Economic and Social Council (ECOSOC), and other forums, it continues to play bloc politics. The disparate approach between India's bilateral and multilateral relations is striking, and it remains unclear which approach India would take as a permanent or long-term member of the UNSC. Today, India, like Brazil and South Africa, has the opportunity to criticize without real global responsibilities. Certainly the experience of China—whose seat in the UN and on the UNSC has been held by the People's Republic of China since 1971—suggests that any process of "socialization" may be gradual, and recommends that permanent-member expansion be based on demonstrated global leadership, including by contributing tangibly to international peace and security, providing global public goods, and defending international rules.[35]

Rights and Responsibilities: A Criteria-Based Approach

Given that U.S. interests in enlargement are riding on the future behavior of aspirant countries, the United States would do well to pursue a disciplined, criteria-based approach to enlargement. Permanent UNSC membership confers both rights and responsibilities. Much is made of the privileges—a permanent seat in the discussion of all major security issues, possible veto power over UNSC actions, and seats on various UN technical agency boards.[36] Less attention is paid (including by some aspirants) to the obligations inherent in permanent membership, which implies serving as a guarantor of international peace. Indeed, the UN Charter implies expectations against which to judge aspirant candidacies. These include above all a unique commitment and capacity to defend international law, preserve regional and global stability, prevent and resolve violent conflicts, and enforce UNSC decisions, including with sanctions and military assets if required.

Given these expectations, reasonable criteria or qualifications for permanent membership, consistent with the charter, might include some mixture of the following:

- a history of political stability, ideally including a commitment to democratic values;
- a globally or regionally deployable military, relevant civilian capabilities, and a willingness to put them at the United Nations' disposal or to use them pursuant to a UNSC resolution;
- financial contributions to the United Nations' regular budget, including a potential percentage threshold for permanent members (see Appendix 5);
- financial contributions to UN peacekeeping and other multilateral operations (see Appendix 5);
- demonstrated willingness to use, when appropriate, the tools that are reserved to the UNSC under UN Charter Chapter VII, including sanctions, force, international intervention, etc.;

- an ability to lead and broker sometimes unpopular global and regional solutions, to promote collective action (as demonstrated in multilateral negotiations, peace talks, global initiatives, good offices, etc.), and to balance regional and domestic decisions when warranted;
- the diplomatic ability to staff and lead an increasingly taxing UNSC agenda, both in New York and globally; and
- a record of conforming to and enforcing global security regimes (including nonproliferation regimes), and contributing to other global public goods.

At present, it is hard to identify any aspirant country that could meet all these criteria (see Appendix 6). Indeed, some current permanent members would have difficulty fulfilling them all. No doubt, the relevant criteria would need to be debated, sharpened, and refined in domestic U.S. and multilateral deliberations.

Proposing a criteria-based approach, however, would usefully shift the focus of conversation from entitlement to qualifications, without a priori excluding any aspirant. In so doing, it would provide a baseline to assess candidates, grant greater transparency to the reform path, and encourage aspirants to exercise globally responsible behavior in international institutions. This approach would also steer negotiations away from framework proposals that leave the selection of permanent members to regional groupings. The United States might consider coupling criteria-based and long-term membership approaches, effectively creating an interim status in which aspirants could prove their bona fides before the UNGA votes on permanent status.

There is, of course, no guarantee that once a country gained permanent membership it would continue to fulfill its obligations. But such a criteria-based approach would provide a clear set of benchmarks by which a country's policies and behaviors could continue to be reassessed. It could also serve the broader purpose of reminding current permanent members, notably Russia and China, of the expectations inherent in their positions under the UN Charter.

Regardless of whether enlargement occurs in the near or long term, openness to a modest expansion of the Security Council based on clearly defined criteria could serve U.S. interests by preempting deleterious enlargement schemes and by redefining the terms of the debate. Establishing a moral high ground could also pay diplomatic dividends for the United States in multilateral forums, as it seeks out areas for cooperation with aspirant countries to demonstrate their increased ownership and responsibility in addressing global threats. In addition, U.S. advocacy for enlargement could result in improved bilateral relations with major aspirant countries.

Recommendations for U.S. Policy

President Obama rightly argues that the world's main international institutions should be adapted to the realities of the twenty-first century.[37] This vision of a reformed international architecture will be incomplete without consideration of the United Nations and its Security Council. Altering the UNSC's composition has the potential to advance U.S. interests if the reform adheres to certain parameters of size and effectiveness, and if it harnesses emerging powers to global effect.

At present, none of the major proposals for UNSC enlargement satisfy these two ifs. Without significant concessions from the major negotiating blocs, there seems little prospect for a reform formula that does—particularly regarding UNSC size—while garnering two-thirds support in the UNGA. Nor is there sufficient evidence that major aspirants are prepared as yet to accept the obligations of permanent (or long-term) membership. But a change in the current constellation of interests—such as newfound flexibility in G4 policy or a fracturing of the Africa consensus—could spark new momentum in the debate.

The skill of the United States to bring about charter reform is untested. Most observers agree that no UNSC enlargement will occur without U.S. leadership, but the United States may not possess sufficient leverage to develop a solution supported by two-thirds of the UNGA and all the P5. It has also been hard for U.S. officials to carve out a position that alienates neither the G4 nor the next tier of influential countries, many of them U.S. allies (including South Korea, Pakistan, and Italy). But if the United States insists on an evolutionary and criteria-based approach, it could galvanize movement for constructive reform while placing the onus on leading aspirants to prove their bona fides.

The risks of taking on the issue—including being blamed for any eventual failure—are admittedly high. The United States has a daunting agenda in New York, and debate over acceptable criteria for UNSC enlargement would affect other U.S. initiatives. But if the risks are significant, so are the potential rewards—namely, an enlargement that more effectively marshals global resources in promoting peace and security. By staking out a positive stance on UNSC expansion, the United States could potentially reap diplomatic rewards, in terms of enhanced relations with leading aspirant states, including some of the world's most important emerging and established countries.

That the UNSC is not currently in crisis plays to the United States' favor in negotiating a measured, criteria-based process for reform. Pressure for UNSC enlargement will likely grow over time, but it is not at present unmanageable. Indeed, the recent presence of several aspirant states (including Japan, Nigeria, Brazil, Turkey, and Mexico, and next year India, South Africa, and Germany) as elected members of the UNSC—as well as the enlargement of the G8 to the G20—has acted as a pressure valve. This lull presents the United States with an opportunity to get its own house in order by sharpening its policy stance; consulting with and preparing the ground in Congress; reaching out to its main allies, P5 counterparts, and the leading aspirants; and building bridges with regional blocs in multilateral settings.

The effort hinges on obtaining allies for a criteria-based reform push. U.S. diplomacy must focus on forging consensus on qualifications for permanent or long-term membership and a process by which aspirant efforts will be measured. The United States must immediately begin to decrease bloc tensions that undermine the candidacy of aspirant countries and increase pressure on the G4, African states, and the UfC for compromise.

Such a strategy, carefully sequenced, allows the United States to be proactive rather than obstructionist, while putting the ball in the court of aspirant countries. It also ensures that when pressure for UNSC reform begins to mount anew, the United States will have shaped the terms of the negotiation. Such an evolutionary strategy minimizes the likelihood that ill-considered enlargement proposals make their way to a vote in the UNGA, while avoiding a precipitous debate on the most divisive issue at the United Nations when the United States must bridge toxic North-South dynamics in New York. In addition, this type of approach avoids proposing a specific enlargement solution until it is clear that a reform in U.S. interests is feasible.

Specifically, the United States should pursue the following steps outlined below.

DECLARE U.S. SUPPORT FOR LIMITED UNSC ENLARGEMENT BASED ON CRITERIA RATHER THAN ENTITLEMENT

At an early date and after interagency deliberations, President Obama should use a high-profile public speech, such as at the UNGA opening session in September 2011, to declare U.S. openness to a modest expansion of the UNSC contingent on demonstrated evidence of aspirants' capacity and willingness to contribute to international peace and security. After initial consultations and agreement with P5 partners by the United States, the president's speech should outline the road map and criteria for this UNSC enlargement, and serve as a launching pad for U.S. consultations with aspirant countries on initiatives that will help them demonstrate the qualifications for permanent membership. Such initiatives might include demonstrating leadership in nonproliferation talks, climate change negotiations, or the advancement of human rights.

REACH EXECUTIVE BRANCH CONSENSUS ON CRITERIA FOR UNSC ENLARGEMENT

To shape the contours of an international agreement that takes a criteria-based, evolutionary approach, the U.S. National Security Council (NSC) should initiate and chair an interagency review led by the State Department and include other relevant entities (such as the Defense and Treasury departments, the U.S. Agency for International Development, and the intelligence agencies). The NSC should also instruct the intelligence agencies to plan potential negotiation scenarios, UNSC compositions (including interim options), likely behavior of aspirant states, and their effects on U.S. interests.

Meanwhile, the interagency committee should identify a draft list of qualifications for evaluating new permanent candidates and a diplomatic strategy to achieve P5 consensus on the criteria. The committee should establish minimum parameters for the U.S. negotiating position (such as no extension of the veto to any new members and a limit to the total number of new members allowed within a certain period). The committee could also consider a charter amendment to allow elected members to serve consecutive terms while aspirant countries work toward fulfilling road map criteria, and whether the UNSC expansion process should be linked to reforms of the wider UN structure.[38]

INITIATE DISCREET DIALOGUE IN CAPITALS WITH THE P5 AND MAJOR ASPIRANT STATES

UNSC enlargement will not be determined in open negotiations in New York. If reform occurs, it will happen through quiet negotiations in the capitals of the P5 and aspirants. Shifting talks from New York to capitals might also clear away some of the mud of acrimonious debates at UN headquarters and allow diplomats to conduct more productive negotiations.

The first step is to garner P5 consensus on an approach to UNSC enlargement based on concrete and transparent criteria, permitting the P5 to emerge as a "credentials committee" of sorts. Any proposal to reform the council will quickly acquire enemies if it bears a "made in the USA" stamp, so a careful sequencing of negotiations is imperative. Washington should seek endorsement from other permanent members for concrete and transparent criteria for permanent membership, as well as explore the potential for long-term, interim seats that might provide an opportunity to gauge aspirant willingness to assume global responsibilities. These conversations should begin with London and Paris, to be followed by discussions with Moscow and Beijing. Achieving consensus is likely to be particularly arduous with China and Russia, whose vision of the UNSC has often been at odds with that of their Western counterparts. At the same time, the history of the 1965 enlargement, as well as recent Russian and Chinese negotiating behavior in New York, suggests that in the end neither country will want to be perceived as standing alone in blocking a UNSC reform effort supported by a majority of member states.

The United States should then use its bilateral strategic dialogues with aspirant countries to present its parameters for UNSC enlargement. This is particularly critical for developing country aspirants like India, Brazil, and South Africa, which, notwithstanding close bilateral relations with the United States, maintain nonaligned stances in New York and Geneva. Jointly with the P5, Washington should present major aspirant countries with a road map for UNSC enlargement that demands greater flexibility in exchange for a clear, evolutionary path toward reform. Washington should include UNSC reform criteria and other multilateral initiatives in its bilateral strategic dialogues with major aspirant countries that might be willing to adjust their bottom line and pursue such a road map if reform is seen to be within their grasp. Beyond establishing the parameters for a successful UNSC reform, U.S. investment in intensified bilateral dialogues with major aspirant countries is likely to pay both immediate and long-term diplomatic dividends.

PREPARE THE GROUND WITH CONGRESS

The Obama administration should immediately initiate discussions with the Senate on U.S. interests in (and criteria for) UNSC reform. This is critical, since any amendment to the UN Charter would require consent by two-thirds of the Senate prior to ratification. Engaging senators from both parties will help ensure that U.S. negotiating goals are grounded in legislative reality—and help avoid repeating mistakes of the past, from the League of Nations to the Kyoto Protocol. Sustained U.S. support for multilateral commitments has always depended on robust bipartisan support in the Senate. With this in mind, the Senate Foreign Relations Committee should convene hearings on this topic with U.S. officials and experts. Such hearings would be useful both diplomatically—by signaling to other countries the limits of U.S. policy flexibility—and domestically—by educating the public on the rationale for any proposed shift in the UNSC structure.

IDENTIFY REFORMS TO UNSC WORKING METHODS THAT ADDRESS TRANSPARENCY CONCERNS

While a discussion of working methods is unlikely to dissuade aspirants from continuing their campaigns, the United States should discuss changes to UNSC operations as part of its reform efforts.[39]

Some reforms have already been implemented—the UNSC publishes its monthly program, hosts more open (as well as closed) meetings, and holds new-member briefings on UNSC procedures. Yet the

UNSC remains a closed and privileged entity, passing resolutions with limited input from states affected by—and expected to implement—them. In an effort to respond to these complaints, the Obama administration has advocated a "nothing about you without you" approach, and has launched several outreach initiatives to non-UNSC members.

Going forward, the Obama administration should identify additional ways to increase transparency and participation into the UNSC's operations. These options include:

- *Expand consultations with countries that contribute peacekeeping troops.* Building on President Obama's meeting with major troop contributors in September 2009, the United States should press the UNSC to hold regular consultations with such countries prior to authorizing or renewing peace operations.[40] The United States should encourage aspirant countries that frequently contribute troops (like South Africa, India, and Brazil) to lead in this venue.
- *Increase transparency of the counterterrorism committees.* The United States should also spearhead reform of the 1540 and 1267 committees—particularly their listing and delisting procedures—to ensure greater transparency and access. The United States should work with committee chairs to determine how committee procedures can be explained to the public, listing processes declassified and adjudication of appeals processed in a timely manner.

At the same time, U.S. officials must remain realistic. Already, the proliferation of UNSC meetings has resulted in a packed agenda that complicates quick action during emergencies, with negotiations sometimes lasting well into the night. Time spent negotiating toothless press and presidential statements after every newsworthy incident could be better spent negotiating an actionable response. Moreover, in dealing with the most sensitive issues on its agenda, the UNSC will inevitably continue to meet in small, closed-door sessions where diplomats can partake in political bargaining with a minimum of political theater.

IDENTIFY ALTERNATIVE FORUMS TO ADDRESS LEGITIMACY CONCERNS AND ASSESS ASPIRANT BEHAVIOR

Finally, the United States should identify other international forums that can provide greater input from emerging powers and increased regional parity in global governance, while also serving as a proving ground for improved North-South cooperation. The elevation of the G20 as the premier steering group for the global economy is particularly significant in this regard. By bringing rising powers into the inner sanctum, the G20 has at least temporarily eased pressure on the UNSC expansion debate. Moreover, it has done so while providing a setting to gauge those countries' willingness to help provide global public goods and a potential venue to build shared understanding of major global threats.

Likewise, the Major Economies Forum has given emerging powers a seat at the table in the leading multilateral forum outside the UN Framework Convention on Climate Change. Within the UN system, there is vast room for aspirant country leadership in improving the workings and results of such bodies as the UN Human Rights Council and the Economic and Social Council. The United States should use such frameworks as testing grounds for emerging power behavior and create "minilateral" forums for other global issues, even as it contemplates UNSC reform.

Conclusion

The UNSC remains an indispensable pillar of world order in the twenty-first century. But to ensure global security and advance U.S. national interests, the UNSC must be able to draw on the resources of the world's most powerful countries. In its effort to update and improve the architecture of global cooperation, the Obama administration must not exclude the world's premier body for international security.

Now is the time to lay the groundwork for UNSC reform—while the United States remains the world's most powerful nation with unparalleled capacity to shape the debate. The first steps in this process will be launching an interagency analysis of reform scenarios and their implications for U.S. interests, building consensus with P5 partners on criteria for additional permanent (or a new category of long-term) membership, consulting Congress on the parameters of U.S. policy toward reform, and building confidence in New York and the P5 capitals to secure the buy-in of major aspirants to a criteria-based reform process.

President Obama's vocal desire to renovate the building blocks of international cooperation and his focus on improving relations for multilateral diplomacy present an opportunity to promote a disciplined and transparent approach to a renovated UNSC. The Obama administration should seize this moment. By expending political capital now, the United States can shift the focus of the UNSC enlargement narrative from entitlement to responsibility, spur better multilateral cooperation in the near term, and lead the negotiation toward a modest expansion that advances the United States' interests in the long run.

Appendix 1: Shifting Global Economic and Military Power*

REAL GDP, GLOBAL RANK, 1945†

1.	*United States*	$1,645 billion
2.	*United Kingdom*	$347 billion
3.	*Soviet Union*	$334 billion
4.	Germany	$302 billion
5.	India	$273 billion
6.	Japan	$103 billion
7.	*France*	$102 billion
8.	Canada	$88 billion
9.	Italy	$87 billion
10.	Argentina	$67 billion

DEFENSE SPENDING, 1955

	Country	Defense spending
1.	*United States*	$40.5 billion
2.	*Soviet Union*	$29.5 billion
3.	*United Kingdom*	$4.3 billion
4.	*France*	$2.9 billion
5.	*China*	$2.5 billion
6.	West Germany	$1.7 billion
7.	Italy	$0.8 billion
8.	Japan	$0.4 billion

*Permanent UNSC members in italics.

†No data available for China in 1945.

NOMINAL GDP, GLOBAL RANK, 2008

1. *United States* $14,441 billion
2. Japan $4,911 billion
3. *China* $4,327 billion
4. Germany $3,673 billion
5. *France* $2,867 billion
6. *United Kingdom* $2,680 billion
7. Italy $2,314 billion
8. *Russia* $1,677 billion
9. Spain $1,602 billion
10. Brazil $1,573 billion

DEFENSE SPENDING, 2008–2009

1. *United States* $607 billion
2. *China* $84.9 billion
3. *France* $65.7 billion
4. *United Kingdom* $65.3 billion
5. *Russia* $58.6 billion
6. Germany $46.8 billion
7. Japan $46.3 billion
8. Italy $40.6 billion
9. Saudi Arabia $38.2 billion
10. India $30.0 billion

Sources: Angus Maddison, "GDP Levels" (University of Groningen: Groningen Growth and Development Centre), www.ggdc.net/maddison/Historical_Statistics/horizontal-file_09-2008.xls; International Monetary Fund, "World Economic Outlook," April 2009, http://www.imf.org/external/pubs/ft/weo/2009/01/; Paul Kennedy, *The Rise and Fall of the Great Powers* (New York: Random House, 1989), p. 384; Stockholm International Peace Research Institute, "The SIPRI Military Expenditure Database," http://milexdata.sipri.org.

Appendix 2: The Council Enlargement of 1965: A Precedent? Or Irrelevant?[41]

The composition of the UN Security Council has changed only once in its sixty-five-year history. In 1963, the General Assembly voted to increase the council's elected members from six to ten, and its overall size from eleven to fifteen states. By 1965, the required number of countries had approved the charter amendment, bringing it into force. How was this charter revision accomplished, and are there any lessons applicable to current reform efforts?

The 1965 expansion occurred in the wake of decolonization and during the Cold War. Prior to enlargement, the six elected UNSC seats were apportioned by informal agreement: two seats to Latin America, one to the British Commonwealth, one to the Middle East, one to Western Europe, and one to Eastern Europe. In 1956, Latin American states proposed expanding nonpermanent members to eight, by adding a seat apiece to Asia and Africa, and by 1960 a number of Western European states had joined this campaign. The Soviet Union refused to consider any UNSC reform, however, as long as the Taiwan-based Nationalist government continued to represent China on the Security Council, alienating emerging nations of the nonaligned movement, who held their first summit in 1960.

In 1963, Latin American, Asian, and African states tried again under the NAM banner, tabling a draft resolution calling for an expansion of elected seats from six to ten, with two apiece for Asia and Africa. Despite abstentions from the United States and Britain (which had both endorsed an expansion to eight rather than ten), and opposition from France and the Soviet Union (which objected to dilution of P5 power), the UNGA adopted Resolution 1991A, 97–11, with only Nationalist China voting for the resolution among the P5. That resolution amended the charter to increase nonpermanent seats from six to ten and established quotas for regional representation. In the aftermath of the UNGA vote, momentum swung quickly toward expansion.

The Soviet Union was the first of the P5 laggards to alter its position, followed in succession by the United Kingdom, the United States, and France.[42] By August 31, 1965, when the amendment entered into force, ninety-five member states had ratified the resolution.

The 1965 expansion holds several insights:

- *The Power of the Nonaligned Movement:* The 1965 expansion revealed the growing power of the emerging NAM bloc in the Cold War context. Decolonization gave birth to a large number of new, non-aligned states that, by banding together, held a voting majority in the UNGA. This majority allowed the movement to force a vote on the charter amendment because it was confident that Britain, France, and the United States would not bear the diplomatic cost of vetoing it. While today's diplomatic landscape is far less cohesive and more heterogeneous (the G77 and NAM are internally divided on UNSC expansion, with influential members in different camps), the 1965 amendment demonstrates that a well-organized bloc of developing countries can press UNSC reform over the reservations of permanent members. Today, the African Union is well positioned to play the role of kingmaker, should it throw its numerical weight behind a reform framework.
- *The Nature of Reform:* The primary force behind expansion in the 1960s was a rapid shift in UN member state demographics—a dynamic that has no contemporary parallel. Between 1956 and 1965, forty-three new nations joined the United Nations—all but seven from Africa and Asia. By 1963, more than half of the countries in the General Assembly (59 out of 113) were Asian, African, or Middle Eastern. Unlike today, the 1960s debate did not consider changes to the permanent membership. Expansion of elected membership addressed the acute underrepresentation of Asia and Africa after decolonization. The expansion thus did not alter the UNSC's permanent membership.
- *The Reluctance of Permanent Members to Stand Alone:* In principle, the requirement for domestic ratification by the P5 provides each with a potential veto over any charter amendment. In practice, the 1963–65 experience suggests diplomatic discomfort in casting a "lonely veto."[43] This has potential relevance for current reform scenarios. If four of the current P5 throw their weight behind an expansion scenario enjoying UNGA support, pressure on the lone dissenter could become intense.

- *The Prospects for Domestic Ratification:* In 1965, the challenge of securing domestic ratification was less daunting than reaching intergovernmental agreement on expansion. This does not hold today. The increase in the number of democracies since 1965, coupled with the controversial proposition of permanent-member-seat reform, will likely raise significant legislative obstacles.

Appendix 3: Overall Voting Coincidence with the United States in the UNGA

A. UN SECURITY COUNCIL ASPIRANTS (NONCONSENSUAL VOTES)

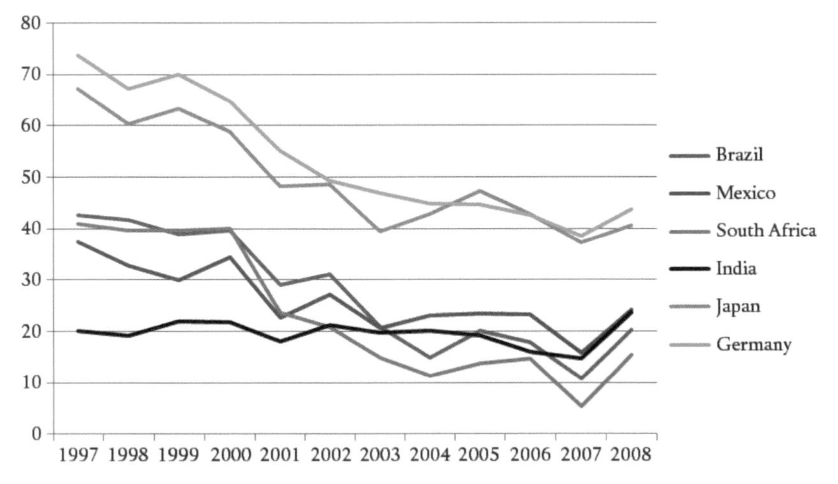

B. PERMANENT MEMBERS (NONCONSENSUAL VOTES)

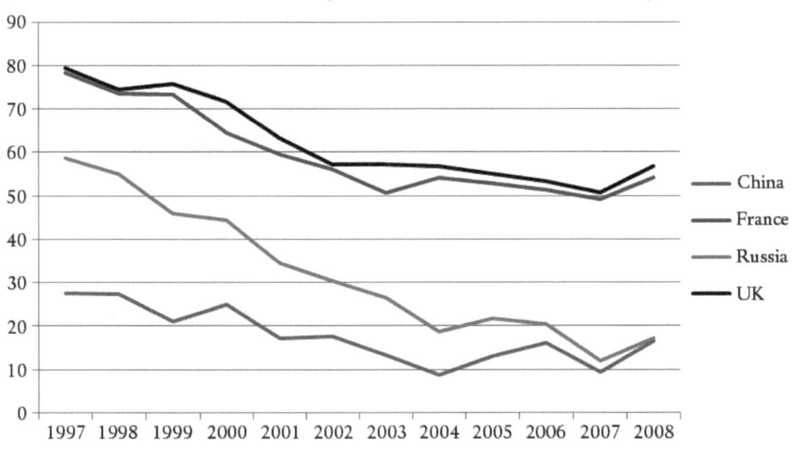

Source: U.S. Department of State, "Voting Practices in the United Nations, 2009," March 2009, http://www.state.gov/p/io/rls/rpt/c36010.htm.

Appendix 4: The Security Council Reform Debate: The Principal Coalitions

COALITION	*PROPOSAL*
Group of Four (G4) Germany, Japan, Brazil, and India	The G4 proposal (A/59/L64, July 2005) would increase the UNSC to twenty-five members by adding six permanent and four nonpermanent members. Asia and Africa would receive two new permanent member seats apiece, and Latin/South America and western Europe one seat each. New nonpermanent seats would be given to Africa, Asia, eastern Europe, and Latin America. The proposal calls for veto rights for new permanent members, though the G4 offered to defer use of the veto for fifteen years, and pending a review conference to discuss the issue. The G4 comprises four democracies—two from the developed and two from the developing world.
Uniting for Consensus (UfC) Led by G4 rivals (Mexico, Italy, South Korea, Pakistan, etc.)	The UfC proposal (A/59/L68, July 2005) would increase UNSC membership to twenty-five by adding ten nonpermanent two-year seats. The twenty elected members would be based on regional representation, with six from Africa, five from Asia, four from the Group of Latin American and Caribbean Countries, three from the Western European and Others Group, and two from east European states. The UfC supports an "intermediate" solution of reelectable seats, without the prospect of permanent status. Membership of the UfC is reported as low as a dozen and as high as forty members.

COALITION	*PROPOSAL*
Africa Bloc Reflects the official position of the African Union	The African proposal (A/60/L41, December 2005) reflects the Ezulwini Consensus agreed upon by African heads of state in July 2005. It would increase the UNSC's size to twenty-six members by adding six permanent and five nonpermanent members. The new permanent members would be distributed consistent with the G4 scheme, but two new elected seats would go to Africa (rather than one), alongside one apiece to the Asian, east European, and Latin American regions. The proposal envisions full veto rights for all new permanent members.

Source: Compiled by authors.

Appendix 5: Leading Contributors to UN Budget, Peacekeeping Budget, and Peacekeeping Forces

SHARE OF CONTRIBUTIONS TO UN REGULAR BUDGET (2008–2009)

Top Ten:

1.	United States	22.00%
2.	Japan	16.62%
3.	Germany	8.58%
4.	United Kingdom	6.64%
5.	France	6.30%
6.	Italy	5.07%
7.	Canada	2.97%
8.	Spain	2.96%
9.	China	2.66%
10.	Mexico	2.25%

Others:

Russia	1.200%
Brazil	0.876%
India	0.450%
South Africa	0.290%
Nigeria	0.048%

SHARE OF CONTRIBUTIONS TO UN PEACEKEEPING BUDGET (2008–2009)

Top Ten:

1.	United States	25.96%
2.	Japan	16.62%
3.	Germany	8.58%
4.	United Kingdom	7.84%
5.	France	7.44%

6.	Italy	5.07%
7.	China	3.15%
8.	Canada	2.98%
9.	Spain	2.97%
10.	South Korea	2.17%
Others:		
	Russia	1.41%
	Brazil	0.18%
	India	0.09%
	South Africa	0.06%
	Nigeria	0.0096%

TOP TEN TROOP CONTRIBUTORS TO UN PEACE OPERATIONS (2009)

1.	Pakistan	10,605
2.	Bangladesh	10,282
3.	India	8,759
4.	Nigeria	5,905
5.	Nepal	4,348
6.	Egypt	4,140
7.	Rwanda	3,683
8.	Jordan	3,669
9.	Ghana	3,398
10.	Italy	2,666

Sources: United Nations Secretariat, *Assessment of Member States' Contributions to the United Nations Regular Budget for the Year 2009*, ST/ADM/SER.B/755 (December 4, 2008); UN Department of Peacekeeping, "Department of Field Support," http://www.un.org/en/peacekeeping/dfs.shtml; UN Department of Peacekeeping, "Fact Sheet; UN General Assembly, *Implementation of General Assembly Resolution 55/235 and 55/236*, A/64/220* (September 23, 2009); UN Committee on Contributions, *Status of Contributions as at 31 December 2008*, ST/ADM/SER.B/761 (December 31, 2008); UN Department of Peacekeeping, "Ranking of Military and Police Contributions to UN Operations," October 31, 2009, http// www.un.org/en/peacekeeping/contributors/2009/oct09_2.pdf.

Appendix 6: Evaluating the Main Aspirants to Permanent Membership

JAPAN

STRENGTHS

- Reliable U.S. ally, including on votes in the UNGA and UNSC
- High share of assessed contributions to UN budget and peacekeeping budget
- Strong diplomatic core
- Established democracy
- Economic power

WEAKNESSES

- Modest military power
- Constitutional prohibition on war

GERMANY

STRENGTHS

- Reliable U.S. ally, including on votes in the UNGA and UNSC
- High share of assessed contributions to UN budget and peacekeeping budget
- Major troop contributor to peace operations (UN and other)
- Strong diplomatic core
- Established military capability and NATO ally
- Established democracy
- Economic power

WEAKNESSES

- Political/historical constraints on use of force
- Overrepresentation of Europe among permanent members

INDIA

STRENGTHS

- Frequent U.S. partner
- Major troop contributor to UN peace operations
- Growing military capability, including naval
- Strong diplomatic core
- Established democracy
- Fast-rising economy
- Large population

WEAKNESSES

- Leader of NAM and G77 ideology in multilateral settings; limits U.S. partnership
- Limited contribution to UN regular budget and peacekeeping budget
- Difficult regional neighborhood
- Ongoing border dispute
- Problematic nuclear policy

BRAZIL

STRENGTHS

- Frequent U.S. partner
- Major troop contributor to UN peace operations in the region
- Growing (though still modest) military capability
- Strong diplomatic core
- Established democracy
- Rising power
- Dominant regional player
- Large population

WEAKNESSES

- Leader of G77 ideology in multilateral settings; limits U.S. partnership
- Modest contributions to UN budget and peacekeeping budget

SOUTH AFRICA

STRENGTHS

- Democracy (recent)
- Dominant regional leader

WEAKNESSES

- Leader of NAM and G77 ideology in multilateral settings; limits U.S. partnership
- Modest diplomatic corps
- Modest military force projection
- Modest population
- Internal challenges of democratic consolidation

NIGERIA

STRENGTHS

- Major troop contributor to UN peace operations
- Democracy (fragile)
- Regional leader
- Large population

WEAKNESSES

- Subscribes to NAM and G77 ideology in multilateral settings; limits U.S. partnership
- Limited capacity of diplomatic corps
- Limited military force projection
- Uncertain political future, given weak governance, instability, and conflict
- Weak economy
- Sustained regional power in question

Source: Compiled by authors.

Endnotes

1. The White House, National Security Strategy, May 2010, p. 1, http://www.whitehouse.gov/sites/default/files/rss_viewer/national_security_strategy.pdf.
2. Barack Obama, speech delivered to the United Nations General Assembly, September 23, 2009, http://www.whitehouse.gov/the_press_office/Remarks-by-the-President-to-the-United-Nations-General-Assembly. See also Secretary of State Hillary Clinton, "Foreign Policy Address," speech delivered at the Council on Foreign Relations, July 15, 2009, http://www.state.gov/secretary/rm/2009a/july/126071.htm; and Susan E. Rice, "A New Course in the World, A New Approach at the UN," speech delivered at New York University's Center for Global Affairs and Center on International Cooperation, August 12, 2009, http://www.archive.usun.state.gov/press_releases/20090812_163.html.
3. Charter of the United Nations, Chapter V, Article 23.
4. Indeed, the UN Human Rights Council shows that reform can do more harm than good.
5. UN Department of Peacekeeping, "Current Operations," http://www.un.org/en/peacekeeping/currentops.shtml.
6. In a public and rancorous fight for membership in 2006, for example, Venezuela spent millions of dollars on development projects in countries willing in exchange to support its candidacy, and doled out state visits in exchange for support of its campaign.
7. To be sure, other considerations motivated the selection of the P5, particularly France and China. British prime minister Winston Churchill insisted—over the initial objections of U.S. president Franklin D. Roosevelt and Soviet premier Joseph Stalin—that France be elevated into the ranks of the great powers, despite its ignominious defeat in 1940. Likewise, Roosevelt insisted on the inclusion of Nationalist China (despite widespread acknowledgment of its internal turmoil and meager military resources) on the grounds that the UNSC needed at least one permanent member from Asia. See Robert C. Hilderbrand, *Dumbarton Oaks: The Origins of the United Nations* (Chapel Hill: University of North Carolina, 1990).
8. The UNSC's work has also expanded into humanitarian and social areas perceived to be connected with international security. Examples include the issue of HIV/AIDS or the resolutions stressing the critical role of women in peace-building.
9. For a discussion of this strategic logic, see G. John Ikenberry, *After Victory: Institutions, Strategic Restraint, and the Rebuilding of Order after Major Wars* (Princeton: Princeton University Press, 2001).
10. Although the League of Nations suffered from many debilities, among the most crippling was the absence of major powers from the League Council during much of its history.
11. The process is outlined in Chapter XVIII, Articles 108–109, of the UN Charter.
12. In 1964, two-thirds of the UNGA was equivalent to 75 member states; today, it is 126 members. In 1965, several amendments were passed, including enlarging the Security

Council, changing the number of votes needed for a UN Security Council decision, and enlarging the membership of ECOSOC. There were also two later amendments: On June 1968, Article 109 was amended, modifying the majority required in the Security Council for the convening of a review conference. On September 24, 1973, ECOSOC was expanded from twenty-seven to fifty-four members, pursuant to the 1971 UNGA adoption of an amendment to Article 61.

13. United Nations Secretariat, Assessment of Member States' Contributions to the United Nations Regular Budget for the Year 2009, ST/ADM/SER.B/755 (December 4, 2008). Ambivalence over what the United States receives in exchange for its $598 million contribution to the UN budget also persists among U.S. taxpayers.
14. In a 2008 CCGA poll, 66 percent of Americans polled favored adding Germany and 67 percent favored adding Japan as permanent members. A majority of Americans also supported permanent membership for India and Brazil, albeit at the lower level of 53 percent for both countries. A plurality of respondents (47 percent) supported South Africa's candidacy. For a compilation of recent poll results from 2005 to 2008, see "Chapter 10: U.S. Opinion on International Institutions," Public Opinion on Global Issues (Washington, DC: Council on Foreign Relations, 2009), http://www.cfr.org/publicopinion.
15. In December 1993, the UNGA passed Resolution 48/26, establishing an "Open-ended Working Group to Consider All Aspects of the Question of Increase in the Membership of the Security Council, and Other Matters Related to the Security Council," but the debate largely languished in this body for the next decade.
16. Annan's report, including options for Security Council reform, was heavily influenced by the report of the High Level Panel on Threats, Challenges, and Change, released in December 2004. He proposed two models to expand the UNSC from fifteen to twenty-four members. Model A reflected the predilections of the four main aspirants to permanent membership—the so-called G4 countries (Germany, Japan, India, and Brazil). It envisioned six new permanent seats, including two for Asia, two for Africa, and one apiece for Europe and the Americas. Model B was tailored to appeal to the so-called Uniting for Consensus (UfC) group, led by Italy, South Korea, Pakistan, Argentina, and Mexico. It called for eight new members in a new category of four-year renewable seats, plus one additional elected member.
17. What is perhaps most striking about the negotiating landscape is that for an enlargement based seemingly on improving regional parity on the council, regional blocs are themselves widely split on reform solutions. Aspiring members actually find their biggest problems in marshaling support from their own blocs.
18. The shift to intergovernmental negotiations in the UNGA plenary raises the prospect that an enlargement resolution could be brought to a vote absent consensus. These intergovernmental negotiations have been chaired by the Afghan permanent representative Zahir Tanin and have debated categories of UNSC membership in any expansion; the question of regional representation; proposals to extend (or restrict) the veto; steps to reform the UNSC's working methods; and the relationship between the UNSC and the UNGA. UN member states held five negotiating sessions through October 2010.
19. The two released a joint statement on March 27, 2008, reaffirming their commitment to the candidacy of the G4 countries. Joint UK-France Summit Declaration, March 27, 2008, http://www.number10.gov.uk/Page15144.
20. The full quotation from Susan E. Rice's confirmation hearings is, "Let me offer, Mr. Chairman, some sense of the principles that will guide the United States during this process. First, we start from a straightforward premise: The United States believes that the long-term legitimacy and viability of the United Nations Security Council depends on its reflecting the world of the twenty-first century. As such, we will make a

serious, deliberative effort, working with partners and allies, to find a way forward that enhances the ability of the Security Council to carry out its mandate and effectively meet the challenges of the new century. I would note that the United States is not linking Security Council reform to other aspects of UN reform. We view both as important and will pursue them in tandem. I would also note that we support expansion of the Security Council in a way that will not diminish its effectiveness or its efficiency. And finally, the United States will take into account the ability of countries to contribute to the maintenance of international peace and security, and the other purposes of the United Nations." Statement by Ambassador Susan E. Rice, U.S. permanent representative to the United Nations, at an informal meeting of the General Assembly on Security Council Reform, February 19, 2009, http://www.usun.state.gov/briefing/statements/2009/february/127091.htm.

21. Most proposals for adding permanent seats to the UNSC tabled to date have been framework proposals—that is, they propose that permanent seats be allocated to regions, without identifying a specific country. The rivalries between some aspirant countries have led some reformers to propose that regional blocs be left to determine their own permanent representative, in effect shifting decisions on UNSC membership from the UNGA (as mandated in the UN Charter) to regional blocs. This introduces a wild card in regional negotiations over UNSC reform. It raises the prospect that deadlock, say, between Brazil or Mexico for the seat for Latin and South America could result in an unexpected compromise candidate, a common twist in UN regional negotiations. Although the likelihood is remote, Cuba or Venezuela could conceivably secure a permanent seat—clearly an unacceptable outcome for the United States. To avoid such a possibility, the United States should ensure that any charter amendment altering the UNSC's permanent composition identify future permanent members by name, as the charter did for the original P5.
22. The complete statement of Alejandro Wolff, deputy U.S. permanent representative to the United Nations, was, "The United States is open, in principle, to a limited expansion of both permanent and nonpermanent members. In terms of categories of membership, the United States strongly believes that any consideration of permanent members must be country-specific in nature. In determining which countries merit permanent membership, we will take into account the ability of countries to contribute to the maintenance of international peace and security and other purposes of the United Nations. As we have previously stated, the United States is not open to an enlargement of the Security Council by a charter amendment that changes the current veto structure. To enhance the prospects for success, whatever formula that emerges for an expansion of council membership should have in mind charter requirements for ratification. We remain committed to a serious, deliberate effort, working with other member states, to find a way forward that both adapts the Security Council to current global realities and enhances the ability of the Security Council to carry out its mandate and effectively meet the challenges of the new century." Statement by Ambassador Alejandro Wolff, U.S. deputy permanent representative, in the General Assembly, on the Security Council Report and Security Council Reform, November 13, 2009, http://usun.state.gov/briefing/statements/2009/131936.htm.
23. The White House, "Remarks by the President to the Joint Session of the Indian Parliament in New Delhi, India," November 8, 2010, http://www.whitehouse.gov/the-press-office/2010/11/08/remarks-president-joint-session-indian-parliament-new-delhi-india. Japan's candidacy for permanent membership has enjoyed presidential-level support from four administrations: Nixon, Carter, Clinton, and George W. Bush. Officials of the Eisenhower and Johnson administrations also expressed support, but at a lower level. President Richard Nixon first publicly endorsed a Japanese

seat on the council in a 1973 meeting with Japanese prime minister Kakuei Tanaka. The Ford, Reagan, and George H.W. Bush administrations did not push for Japanese membership. Support revived under President Clinton, who also endorsed Germany's accession to permanent membership in January 1993, and at the outset of the UN's Open-Ended Working Group in 1994. See also Reinhard Drifte, *Japan's Quest for a UN Security Council Seat: A Matter of Pride or Justice* (New York: St. Martin's Press, 2000). The administration of George W. Bush declined to support the G4 proposal in its second term but did support a seat for Japan. As Secretary of State Condoleezza Rice explained, "Japan has earned its honorable place among the nations of the world by its own effort and its own character. That's why the United States unambiguously supports a permanent seat for Japan in the United Nations Security Council."

24. The United States has traditionally spoken of a "modest expansion" of no more than four to six new members.
25. UN Department of Peacekeeping, "Department of Field Support," http://www.un.org/en/peacekeeping/dfs.shtml; UN Department of Peacekeeping, "Fact Sheet," http://www.un.org/en/peacekeeping/ documents/factsheet.pdf.
26. The United States pays approximately 25 percent of UN peacekeeping costs and 22 percent of the UN annual budget.
27. As occurred when the United States proposed an arms embargo on Myanmar in the wake of the latter's crackdown on peaceful demonstrators in August 2007. Due in large part to a threat of Chinese and Russian vetoes, the UNSC instead passed a presidential statement eight weeks later. UNSC presidential statements and press statements are unanimous.
28. The UNSC's only recourse to Iran's continued nuclear program, for example, is to publicize the breaches and to negotiate further measures.
29. Adam Roberts and Dominik Zaum, *Selective Security: War and the United Nations Security Council Since 1945*, Adelphi Paper 395 (London: International Institute for Strategic Studies, 2008).
30. Charter of the United Nations, Chapter V, Article 27.
31. During 2009, the United States could generally count on a blocking coalition of seven votes, and obtaining nine votes was typically within reach. The United States could generally count on the support not only of France and the United Kingdom but also of elected members Austria, Burkina Faso, Costa Rica, Japan, and Uganda, with Croatia and Mexico often following suit. This allowed the United States, France, and the United Kingdom to focus on ensuring that the Chinese and Russians would not use their vetoes. Frequently, the P5 would agree on resolution language and then share the draft with the rest of the UNSC for final negotiations and a vote. In 2010, the diplomatic lineup has been less auspicious for U.S. interests. Burkina Faso and Costa Rica, two staunch U.S. allies, were replaced by Gabon and Nigeria, which, while friends of the United States, frequently represent southern bloc interests, as does newly elected member Brazil. The United States now enters more negotiations potentially short of the nine votes needed for action.
32. While the precise voting formula would be subject to negotiation, the current UNSC configuration, as well as other leading proposals (including the UfC initiative and the UNSC configuration proposed by the UNGA president in 1997) all follow a two-thirds-minus-one formula (that is, approval for a council resolution requires two-thirds of council members, minus one). In a council of twenty-one members, two-thirds minus one would be thirteen votes, but the only proposal with twenty-one members (Panama Proposal) does not specifically list a number of votes needed to pass a resolution.
33. The UfC proposal, which calls for twenty elected members on a twenty-five member UNSC, is especially worrisome, requiring calls for fifteen votes (assuming no vetoes) for a resolution to pass, and only eleven to block. Presumably, U.S. policymakers will

want to avoid any scenario that significantly tilts the balance of seats from permanent to elected members, which has already shifted once (in 1963) from an initial ratio of 5:6 to the current ratio of 5:10. Under the G4 proposal, the ratio would be 11:14; under the UfC proposal, it would be 5:20. But even the G4 option carries some risks in this regard. In a UNSC of twenty-four members, as Secretary-General Kofi Annan proposed in 2005, it is likely that fifteen votes would be needed to pass a resolution, and ten to block.

34. President Barack Obama, "Remarks by the President to the United Nations General Assembly," September 23, 2009, http://www.whitehouse.gov/the_press_office/Remarks-by-the-President-to-the-United-Nations-General-Assembly.
35. James Traub, "At the World's Summit: How Will Leading Nations Lead?" Policy Analysis Brief, Stanley Foundation, 2009.
36. In addition to their role as permanent members, the P5 enjoy other privileges. They are automatically five of the twenty-one vice presidents of the UNGA General Committee. And while there is no formal requirement for P5 participation in any other UN principal agency or organ, the P5 are overrepresented throughout the United Nations. This includes in UNGA ad hoc committees and subsidiary organs (such as the International Law Commission, the Consultative Committee on Disarmament, and the Special Committee on Peacekeeping Operations); on the Economic and Social Council (where the P5 have resided almost continuously since it began); in the International Court of Justice; and in UN programs and agencies (including on the executive boards of the International Atomic Energy Agency; Food and Agriculture Organization; UN Educational, Scientific, and Cultural Organization; UN Children's Fund; and UN Development Program).
37. As the recent National Security Strategy declares, "International institutions must more effectively represent the world of the 21st century, with a broader voice—and greater responsibilities—for emerging powers." The White House, National Security Strategy, p. 3.
38. This could include, for example, reforms to create weighted voting in the UNGA and fifth budgetary committee, which might balance any dilution of U.S. power in the UNSC.
39. To date, the most influential proposals for injecting greater transparency and accountability into UNSC deliberations and decision-making have come from the so-called S5 coalition of small member states. Among other things, the S5 envision improved communication between the UNSC and other UN member states; regular conversations between the UNSC and troop-contributing countries before and after mandates are authorized; enhanced consultations with countries experiencing difficulties as a result of implementing sanctions resolutions and limits on the use of the veto, including not to employ it in cases of "genocide, crimes against humanity, and serious violations of international law." Other S5 proposals, particularly adjustments to the veto, have been more problematic. There is little support among any of the P5 for restrictions on the veto or for charter amendments limiting its use. P5 countries note that the veto privilege remains, as it has since 1945, the price the world's most powerful nations demand for accepting a system of global collective security. Actual use of the veto is increasingly rare—from 2005 to 2009, 94 percent of resolutions passed by consensus, and most of the rest were split votes, with less than 1 percent of the total being vetoed. And when they are used, P5 countries explain their rationale in for-the-record explanations of vote that traditionally occur after a contentious vote. At the same time, the veto is hardly irrelevant. China and Russia have become quite effective at using implicit threats to block U.S.- and European-supported actions, on crises ranging from Kosovo to Iran, Darfur, Myanmar, Zimbabwe, and Sri Lanka.
40. Making such consultation standard practice will require a more organized UNSC agenda that anticipates upcoming peace agreements, includes meetings with host and

contributing countries as a matter of course, and ensures that mandates are both realistic and adequately resourced.

41. The data in this appendix is drawn from: Olivia Lau, "UN Security Council Expansion: The Efficacy of Small States Under Bipolarity and Uni-Multipolarity," October 2003, http://people.iq.harvard.edu/~olau/papers/unreform.pdf; Dimitris Bourantonis, *The History and Politics of U.N. Security Council Reform* (Milton Park: Routledge, 2005); Norman J. Padelford, "Politics and Change in the Security Council," International Organizations 14 (1960); Carolyn L. Willson, "Changing the Charter: The United Nations Prepares for the Twenty-first Century," *The American Journal of International Law,* vol. 90, no. 1 (January 1996), pp. 115–26.
42. Edward C. Luck, "Reforming the United Nations: Lessons from a History in Progress," International Relations Studies and the United Nations Occasional Papers No. 1, Academic Council of the United Nations, 2003, pp. 7–10. Luck contends that the "precarious financial position" of the United Nations, as well as the threat of a Soviet departure from the organization, was an important factor in the U.S. reversal on UNSC expansion.
43. Ibid, p. 9.

About the Authors

Kara C. McDonald is a Foreign Service officer with the U.S. Department of State, and currently serves as the U.S. deputy special coordinator for Haiti. McDonald was an international affairs fellow from 2009 to 2010 and director for United Nations and international operations at the National Security Council from 2007 to 2009. She served as acting senior director for democracy, human rights, and international organizations during the transition to the Obama administration. Prior to serving at the White House, she was a special assistant to R. Nicholas Burns, former undersecretary for political affairs at the State Department, where she advised on African affairs and the United Nations, including negotiations in the Security Council on Iran, North Korea, Lebanon, Sudan, Iraq, Afghanistan, Myanmar, and Kosovo. From 2004 to 2006, McDonald was deputy director for planning in the Office of the Coordinator for Reconstruction and Stabilization (S/CRS) at the Department of State. She has served in and advised on multilateral operations and complex contingencies for more than ten years, and chaired interagency policy committees on peacekeeping and peace-building operations, strategy in the multilateral environment, aid effectiveness, and governance in postconflict. Prior to joining the Department of State, McDonald managed elections and political process assistance to central and eastern Europe for the U.S. Agency for International Development. Her overseas assignments have included Romania, Kosovo, Bosnia-Herzegovina, Haiti, Macedonia, and Croatia. She holds a BA in French and comparative literature from the University of Michigan and an MA from the Fletcher School of Law and Diplomacy at Tufts University. She speaks French and Romanian.

Stewart M. Patrick is senior fellow and director of the International Institutions and Global Governance program at the Council on Foreign Relations. His areas of expertise include multilateral cooperation in the management of global issues; U.S. policy toward international institutions, including the United Nations; and the challenges posed by fragile states. From 2005 to April 2008, he was a research fellow at the Center for Global Development, where he focused on the linkages between state weakness and transnational threats. He also served as a professorial lecturer in international relations/conflict management at Johns Hopkins University's School of Advanced International Studies. From September 2002 to January 2005, Patrick served on the secretary of state's policy planning staff, with lead staff responsibility for U.S. policy toward Afghanistan and a range of global and transnational issues. He joined the State Department as a Council on Foreign Relations international affairs fellow. Prior to government service, Patrick was an associate at the Center on International Cooperation at New York University from 1997 to 2002. He graduated from Stanford University and received his doctorate in international relations, as well as two MA degrees, from Oxford University, where he was a Rhodes scholar. He is the author of *The Best Laid Plans: The Origins of American Multilateralism and the Dawn of the Cold War* and of the forthcoming *Weak Links: Fragile States, Global Threats, and International Security.*

Advisory Committee

Elliott Abrams, *ex officio*
Council on Foreign Relations

Michael Barnett
University of Minnesota

Donald Blinken
European Institute, Columbia University

Christopher W. Brody
Vantage Partners, LLC

R. Nicholas Burns
Harvard Kennedy School

Chester Crocker
Georgetown University

Barbara Crossette
The Nation; UNA-USA

Kim G. Davis
Charlesbank Capital Partners, LLC

Paula J. Dobriansky
Thomson Reuters

Bruce S. Gelb
Council of American Ambassadors

Michael J. Glennon
Fletcher School of Law and Diplomacy

Rita E. Hauser
Hauser Foundation, Inc.

Charlotte Ku
University of Illinois

Ellen Laipson
Henry L. Stimson Center

Edward C. Luck
International Peace Institute

Princeton N. Lyman, *ex officio*
Council on Foreign Relations

Cappy R. McGarr
United States Renewable Energy Group

Donald F. McHenry
Georgetown University

George E. Moose
United States Institute of Peace

Thomas R. Pickering
Hills & Company

Richard Schifter

Stephen C. Schlesinger
Century Foundation

Kristen Silverberg
Vorbeck Materials

Paul B. Stares, *ex officio*
Council on Foreign Relations

James Traub
New York Times Magazine

Richard S. Williamson
Northwestern University

Micah Zenko, *ex officio*
Council on Foreign Relations

This report reflects the judgments and recommendations of the author(s). It does not necessarily represent the views of members of the advisory committee, whose involvement in no way should be interpreted as an endorsement of the report by either themselves or the organizations with which they are affiliated.

Mission Statement of the International Institutions and Global Governance Program

The International Institutions and Global Governance (IIGG) program at CFR aims to identify the institutional requirements for effective multilateral cooperation in the twenty-first century. The program is motivated by recognition that the architecture of global governance—largely reflecting the world as it existed in 1945—has not kept pace with fundamental changes in the international system. These shifts include the spread of transnational challenges, the rise of new powers, and the mounting influence of nonstate actors. Existing multilateral arrangements thus provide an inadequate foundation for addressing many of today's most pressing threats and opportunities and for advancing U.S. national and broader global interests.

Given these trends, U.S. policymakers and other interested actors require rigorous, independent analysis of current structures of multilateral cooperation, and of the promises and pitfalls of alternative institutional arrangements. The IIGG program meets these needs by analyzing the strengths and weaknesses of existing multilateral institutions and proposing reforms tailored to new international circumstances.

The IIGG program fulfills its mandate by

- Engaging CFR fellows in research on improving existing and building new frameworks to address specific global challenges—including climate change, the proliferation of weapons of mass destruction, transnational terrorism, and global health—and disseminating the research through books, articles, Council Special Reports, and other outlets;
- Bringing together influential foreign policymakers, scholars, and CFR members to debate the merits of international regimes and frameworks at meetings in New York, Washington, DC, and other select cities;

- Hosting roundtable series whose objectives are to inform the foreign policy community of today's international governance challenges and breed inventive solutions to strengthen the world's multilateral bodies; and
- Providing a state-of-the-art Web presence as a resource to the wider foreign policy community on issues related to the future of global governance.

Council Special Reports

Published by the Council on Foreign Relations

Congress and National Security
Kay King; CSR No. 58, November 2010

Toward Deeper Reductions in U.S. and Russian Nuclear Weapons
Micah Zenko; CSR No. 57, November 2010
A Center for Preventive Action Report

Internet Governance in an Age of Cyber Insecurity
Robert K. Knake; CSR 56, September 2010
An International Institutions and Global Governance Program Report

From Rome to Kampala: The U.S. Approach to the 2010 International Criminal Court Review Conference
Vijay Padmanabhan; CSR No. 55, April 2010

Strengthening the Nuclear Nonproliferation Regime
Paul Lettow; CSR No. 54, April 2010
An International Institutions and Global Governance Program Report

The Russian Economic Crisis
Jeffrey Mankoff; CSR No. 53, April 2010

Somalia: A New Approach
Bronwyn E. Bruton; CSR No. 52, March 2010
A Center for Preventive Action Report

The Future of NATO
James M. Goldgeier; CSR No. 51, February 2010
An International Institutions and Global Governance Program Report

The United States in the New Asia
Evan A. Feigenbaum and Robert A. Manning; CSR No. 50, November 2009
An International Institutions and Global Governance Program Report

Intervention to Stop Genocide and Mass Atrocities: International Norms and U.S. Policy
Matthew C. Waxman; CSR No. 49, October 2009
An International Institutions and Global Governance Program Report

Enhancing U.S. Preventive Action
Paul B. Stares and Micah Zenko; CSR No. 48, October 2009
A Center for Preventive Action Report

The Canadian Oil Sands: Energy Security vs. Climate Change
Michael A. Levi; CSR No. 47, May 2009
A Maurice R. Greenberg Center for Geoeconomic Studies Report

The National Interest and the Law of the Sea
Scott G. Borgerson; CSR No. 46, May 2009

Lessons of the Financial Crisis
Benn Steil; CSR No. 45, March 2009
A Maurice R. Greenberg Center for Geoeconomic Studies Report

Global Imbalances and the Financial Crisis
Steven Dunaway; CSR No. 44, March 2009
A Maurice R. Greenberg Center for Geoeconomic Studies Report

Eurasian Energy Security
Jeffrey Mankoff; CSR No. 43, February 2009

Preparing for Sudden Change in North Korea
Paul B. Stares and Joel S. Wit; CSR No. 42, January 2009
A Center for Preventive Action Report

Averting Crisis in Ukraine
Steven Pifer; CSR No. 41, January 2009
A Center for Preventive Action Report

Congo: Securing Peace, Sustaining Progress
Anthony W. Gambino; CSR No. 40, October 2008
A Center for Preventive Action Report

Deterring State Sponsorship of Nuclear Terrorism
Michael A. Levi; CSR No. 39, September 2008

China, Space Weapons, and U.S. Security
Bruce W. MacDonald; CSR No. 38, September 2008

Sovereign Wealth and Sovereign Power: The Strategic Consequences of American Indebtedness
Brad W. Setser; CSR No. 37, September 2008
A Maurice R. Greenberg Center for Geoeconomic Studies Report

Securing Pakistan's Tribal Belt
Daniel Markey; CSR No. 36, July 2008 (Web-only release) and August 2008
A Center for Preventive Action Report

Avoiding Transfers to Torture
Ashley S. Deeks; CSR No. 35, June 2008

Global FDI Policy: Correcting a Protectionist Drift
David M. Marchick and Matthew J. Slaughter; CSR No. 34, June 2008
A Maurice R. Greenberg Center for Geoeconomic Studies Report

Dealing with Damascus: Seeking a Greater Return on U.S.-Syria Relations
Mona Yacoubian and Scott Lasensky; CSR No. 33, June 2008
A Center for Preventive Action Report

Climate Change and National Security: An Agenda for Action
Joshua W. Busby; CSR No. 32, November 2007
A Maurice R. Greenberg Center for Geoeconomic Studies Report

Planning for Post-Mugabe Zimbabwe
Michelle D. Gavin; CSR No. 31, October 2007
A Center for Preventive Action Report

The Case for Wage Insurance
Robert J. LaLonde; CSR No. 30, September 2007
A Maurice R. Greenberg Center for Geoeconomic Studies Report

Reform of the International Monetary Fund
Peter B. Kenen; CSR No. 29, May 2007
A Maurice R. Greenberg Center for Geoeconomic Studies Report

Nuclear Energy: Balancing Benefits and Risks
Charles D. Ferguson; CSR No. 28, April 2007

Nigeria: Elections and Continuing Challenges
Robert I. Rotberg; CSR No. 27, April 2007
A Center for Preventive Action Report

The Economic Logic of Illegal Immigration
Gordon H. Hanson; CSR No. 26, April 2007
A Maurice R. Greenberg Center for Geoeconomic Studies Report

The United States and the WTO Dispute Settlement System
Robert Z. Lawrence; CSR No. 25, March 2007
A Maurice R. Greenberg Center for Geoeconomic Studies Report

Bolivia on the Brink
Eduardo A. Gamarra; CSR No. 24, February 2007
A Center for Preventive Action Report

After the Surge: The Case for U.S. Military Disengagement from Iraq
Steven N. Simon; CSR No. 23, February 2007

Darfur and Beyond: What Is Needed to Prevent Mass Atrocities
Lee Feinstein; CSR No. 22, January 2007

Avoiding Conflict in the Horn of Africa: U.S. Policy Toward Ethiopia and Eritrea
Terrence Lyons; CSR No. 21, December 2006
A Center for Preventive Action Report

Living with Hugo: U.S. Policy Toward Hugo Chávez's Venezuela
Richard Lapper; CSR No. 20, November 2006
A Center for Preventive Action Report

Reforming U.S. Patent Policy: Getting the Incentives Right
Keith E. Maskus; CSR No. 19, November 2006
A Maurice R. Greenberg Center for Geoeconomic Studies Report

Foreign Investment and National Security: Getting the Balance Right
Alan P. Larson and David M. Marchick; CSR No. 18, July 2006
A Maurice R. Greenberg Center for Geoeconomic Studies Report

Challenges for a Postelection Mexico: Issues for U.S. Policy
Pamela K. Starr; CSR No. 17, June 2006 (Web-only release) and November 2006

U.S.-India Nuclear Cooperation: A Strategy for Moving Forward
Michael A. Levi and Charles D. Ferguson; CSR No. 16, June 2006

Generating Momentum for a New Era in U.S.-Turkey Relations
Steven A. Cook and Elizabeth Sherwood-Randall; CSR No. 15, June 2006

Peace in Papua: Widening a Window of Opportunity
Blair A. King; CSR No. 14, March 2006
A Center for Preventive Action Report

Neglected Defense: Mobilizing the Private Sector to Support Homeland Security
Stephen E. Flynn and Daniel B. Prieto; CSR No. 13, March 2006

Afghanistan's Uncertain Transition From Turmoil to Normalcy
Barnett R. Rubin; CSR No. 12, March 2006
A Center for Preventive Action Report

Preventing Catastrophic Nuclear Terrorism
Charles D. Ferguson; CSR No. 11, March 2006

Getting Serious About the Twin Deficits
Menzie D. Chinn; CSR No. 10, September 2005
A Maurice R. Greenberg Center for Geoeconomic Studies Report

Both Sides of the Aisle: A Call for Bipartisan Foreign Policy
Nancy E. Roman; CSR No. 9, September 2005

Forgotten Intervention? What the United States Needs to Do in the Western Balkans
Amelia Branczik and William L. Nash; CSR No. 8, June 2005
A Center for Preventive Action Report

A New Beginning: Strategies for a More Fruitful Dialogue with the Muslim World
Craig Charney and Nicole Yakatan; CSR No. 7, May 2005

Power-Sharing in Iraq
David L. Phillips; CSR No. 6, April 2005
A Center for Preventive Action Report

Giving Meaning to "Never Again": Seeking an Effective Response to the Crisis in Darfur and Beyond
Cheryl O. Igiri and Princeton N. Lyman; CSR No. 5, September 2004

Freedom, Prosperity, and Security: The G8 Partnership with Africa: Sea Island 2004 and Beyond
J. Brian Atwood, Robert S. Browne, and Princeton N. Lyman; CSR No. 4, May 2004

Addressing the HIV/AIDS Pandemic: A U.S. Global AIDS Strategy for the Long Term
Daniel M. Fox and Princeton N. Lyman; CSR No. 3, May 2004
Cosponsored with the Milbank Memorial Fund

Challenges for a Post-Election Philippines
Catharin E. Dalpino; CSR No. 2, May 2004
A Center for Preventive Action Report

Stability, Security, and Sovereignty in the Republic of Georgia
David L. Phillips; CSR No. 1, January 2004
A Center for Preventive Action Report

To purchase a printed copy, call the Brookings Institution Press: 800.537.5487.
Note: Council Special Reports are available for download from CFR's website, www.cfr.org.
For more information, email publications@cfr.org.